# DILEMMA OF THE NIGERIAN GIRL CHILD

## CONNUBIALITY / MARRIAGE

## Queen Jennifer Ephraim

# DILEMMA OF THE NIGERIAN GIRL CHILD

First published 2019



Published by:

Jennifer Ephraim Foundation

Jabi FCDA Quarters,

Abuja, Nigeria.

www.jenniferephraimfoundation.org

# Table of Contents

# DEDICATION

Dedicated to the Nigerian girl child, who despite the odds, stands tall and shines bright. May this book serve as a reminder of the challenges you face and also as a celebration of your strength and resilience. May it inspire others to join in the fight for your rights and dignity, and may it be a call to action for a better and brighter future for all.

# FOREWORD

Gender is thorny. It creates, shapes and defines interaction among and between males and females. Not minding slippage between equality and parity, gender determines and shapes human interactions, often determining life outcomes for males and females; especially in developing societies such as Nigeria. This book, *Dilemma of the Nigerian Girl Child: Marriage Vs Education* revives the gender debate without recourse to complex academic discourse.

Starting from the premise that girls and boys are born equally but forced into identities that give one gender more recognition and opportunities over the other, this book asserts that *'man's deliberate refusal to pertinently look into, understand and harness the beauty of gender difference has not only resulted in its underutilisation but also in its abuse.'*

The social classification of gender and its impact on life outcomes is manifest in the book's exposition of the tension between girl child education and child marriage. Without dismissing marriage, which most societies revere, this book questions the tendency in some communities to subjugate girl child education to child marriage. Its thoroughly backgrounded argument takes the reader into a journey that spans the history of Nigeria, gender construction across cultures, and the associated tensions.

*Dilemma of the Nigerian Girl Child: Marriage Vs Education* outlines the dangers of child marriages and makes a strong case for girl child education. The core of this short but lucid book is that early marriage should not hobble the Nigerian girl child's education and chances at life. I have no hesitation in recommending it to those interested in gender issues and child education.

**Dr Abdulfatah Ahmed**
**Former Executive Governor**
**Kwara State, Nigeria**

# PREFACE

According to research data, Nigeria is a country of the young with almost half the entire 220 million-strong population (48 percent) currently under the age of 15. The current total for the children under the age of 5 stands at nearly 35 million, while each year at least 7 million babies are born.

*Dilemma of the Nigerian Girl Child* highlights the problems and dangers that the girl child in Nigeria faces. My experiences as a girl child who was raised by a single mother who gave birth to me at the age of 13, gave me the inspiration to write this book, highlight some of the problems faced by the girl child in Nigeria and proffer solutions to these problems.

I thank my mother and other woman who are trail blazers in their various fields and who bring hope and inspiration to the Nigerian Girl Child.

# ACKNOWLEDGEMENT

Dear Readers,

We are proud to present to you our latest book, *Dilemma of the Nigerian Girl Child.* This book has been a labour of love, and we are grateful to everyone who has contributed to making it a reality.

We would like to extend our heartfelt thanks to Samaila Vangawa, Alex Nwankwo and Kingsley Desmond for their invaluable input. Their insights and expertise have added depth and richness to the book, and their contributions have been instrumental to bringing the subject matter to life.

Their dedication and passion for the cause of promoting the rights of the girl child in Nigeria, is truly inspiring. Their unwavering commitment to this cause has been a source of encouragement and motivation to us, and we are deeply grateful for their support.

We are confident that this book will serve as a catalyst for change and will help to raise awareness about the challenges faced by the Nigerian girl child. We thank Samaila Vangawa, Alex Nwankwo and Kingsley Desmond once again for their invaluable contributions; we are honoured to have worked with such a talented and passionate team.

Sincerely,
Queen Jennifer Ephraim

# INTRODUCTION

It is with great honour that we present to you *Dilemma of the Nigerian Girl Child*. This book shines a light on the unique challenges faced by young girls in Nigeria, and their remarkable strength in the face of adversity. Despite facing obstacles such as poverty, discrimination, and limited access to education and healthcare, the Nigerian girl child stands tall and shines bright. Through their resilience and determination, they have proven to be a source of inspiration to us all.

This book seeks to bring to the forefront the plight of the Nigerian girl child and to raise awareness about the difficulties they face. It highlights the obstacles that prevent them from reaching their full potential and sheds light on the solutions that can help to alleviate their struggles. By telling their stories and shining a light on the challenges they face, we hope to inspire others to join in the fight for their rights and dignity.

We believe that the Nigerian girl child is a valuable member of society who deserves to be valued, respected and given the opportunity to reach their full potential. This book is a call to action for a brighter future for all young girls in Nigeria, and we hope that it will inspire change and encourage others to join in the fight for a better tomorrow.

# Chapter One
## The Nigerian Girl Child

The story of the Nigerian girl child has a distinctive twist to it. This is so because of our diverse cultural backgrounds. Nigeria is a country with many ethnic groups; each with a special cultural heritage. Long before the pre-colonial era, these various ethnic groups had their traditional practices that shaped their existence as a people. These practices were the laws that governed the way people responded to customs such as marriage, burial ceremonies, and the social stratification of men and women in families and society.

During that time, records show that most cultures in Nigeria had always been patriarchal; putting the man as head of the family and at the root of family genealogy. The structures of most African cultures therefore invariably led to more emphasis on the male child than their female counterparts. The typical Nigerian girl child was relegated to the background due to some of the factors mentioned above and several others that will be unveiled further in this book.

It is important to take a look at the girl child in precolonial times and how she thrived. Most cultures at that time believed that girls could only play the role of helping their mothers at home so that they could become good housewives like their mothers. The position of women in pre-colonial Nigeria differed in the vast number of ethnic groups in Nigeria. A woman's position varied according to the (1) kinship structure of the group and (2) the role of women within the economic structure of the society.

Common factors among women of different ethnic groups, however included the domestically oriented jobs and the range of economic activities that the societies reserved for women.

Girls in pre-colonial societies held a complementary position to boys, although patrilineal and patriarchal kinship structures as earlier mentioned predominated in Nigerian societies. The kinship group expected women who married into a Yoruba or Igbo patrilineage to give birth to sons to ensure the future of the group. Furthermore, the position of a young wife improved as she grew older, bore children and earned approval from other older wives in the community. She gained assistance from other younger wives as she grew older, thus allowing her to spend less time in the home and more time engaging in activities outside the household. The activities included farming and craft making, which allowed her to provide the material resources needed to care for her family.

It should be noted that some societies in Nigeria like the

Yoruba society offered the greatest opportunities for women to participate in other economic activities such as manufacturing and trade. However, in the far Northern part of the country, things were done differently. There, the fate of the girl child was predominantly decided based on religious beliefs. Women had restricted rights to partake in the economic welfare of their families.

It is important to note that in some societies in Nigeria's early history, the responsibility of a woman to provide for her family included providing the material resources for such care. Women believed that providing such resources showed their responsibility as women and citizens. Their society considered the work the women did as complementary to the work of men, and some women achieved impressive status in the economic and social realms of life.

On the general scale in Africa, relations between women and men were varied, changing, and culturally specific, yet there were some common themes. Most African societies attempted to attain forms of heterarchy, which meant they often created several centres of authority and aspired to establish communities where gender relations between women and men were equitable. Additionally, throughout history, most cultures in Nigeria determined status by the amount of labour a group or individual could control. And, in a historically under-populated continent, this meant that motherhood and giving birth to children were important. The result is that women, as both biological and social mothers and grandmothers were highly respected throughout the history of the continent.

A deeper perusal of the history of Africans shows that the most successful families in the earliest eras were based on family units that situated grandmothers at the centre; a family structure found in many parts of Africa in the early 21st century. Around 5,500 years ago, a small group of Bantu-speaking people migrated from West Africa and over time populated large portions of Africa below the Sahara Desert. Heterarchy and gender equity were features of most Bantu-speaking societies. Their world views were manifested in the matrilineal social structure that most Bantu societies preferred until recent history. Even the earliest empires in Africa, Nubia and Egypt, were organised matrilineally. The West African Sahel empires from 700 CE were also matrilineal, and there is a long history of Muslim African female rulers. However, with the creation of empires and more centralised societies, hierarchy among some societies replaced heterarchy. This change motivated a shift in gender relations; women from elite lineages maintained their status, while other women tended to lose their traditional positions of authority as mothers and elders within their clans.

Overall, the Atlantic slave trade severely challenged heterarchical social relations and threatened women's authority and status in West Africa.

Another element of this period is the transference of African gender relations to the Americans. During the 19th century, as the Europeans arrived in their numbers, they imposed new gender ideologies as they began to structure how the rest of the world viewed Africans. From the so-called White Man's Burden to Social Darwinism, new definitions of the Order placed African women at the bottom. While women played key roles in the long-term history of Africa in ancient times, the Western analysis of African gender dynamics began to inform colonial policies, dominate world opinion and shape academic research.

From pre-colonial times to the early 21st century, the role and status of women in Nigeria have continuously evolved. However, the image of a helpless, oppressed and marginalised group has undermined their proper study and little recognition has been granted to the various integral functions that Nigerian women have performed throughout history. In the pre-colonial period, women played a major role in social and economic activities. Division of labour was along gender lines, and women controlled such occupations as food processing, mat weaving, pottery and cooking. Moreover, the land was communally owned and women had access to it through their husbands or parents. Although a man was the head of the household in a patrilineal system, older women had control of the labour of younger family members.

Women were also central to trade. Among the Yoruba, they were the major figures in long-distance trade, with enormous opportunities for accumulating wealth and acquiring titles. The most successful among them rose to the prestigious chieftaincy title of *Iyalode*, a position of great privilege and power. Long-distance trade was practised among several cultures and was mostly done by women who trekked long distances to trade by barter in most cases.

Things changed drastically with the coming of the colonial masters who ushered in a new social structure that reversed the role of women, and deemed them inferior in terms of roles and responsibilities of heading the family.

# Chapter Two
## Nigerian Girl Child Debacles

Nigerian cultures are seen to be the catalyst that has paved the tough path for the Nigerian girl child. A path that has seen the girl child in Nigeria go through genital mutilation, home arrest, unequal opportunities, child labour, girl-child marriages etc. We can view the discussion of the continued abuse, violence and relegation of women in Nigeria narrowly or broadly as the case may be. From a narrow perspective, customs and tradition are seen as tools used to limit the prospect of the girl child through denial of education by engaging girls in early marriage amongst others. More broadly is the inability of the world to take a definite stand, speak with one voice and fight the menace in unison, in order to liberate the girl child wherever she is; from her disadvantaged position.

In most cases, depending on the political winds, especially in third world countries, the challenges of the girl child resonates with silken words that seem like the issue would be tackled out rightly, and the desired result achieved in no time. With the fashioned regulative apparatus and high-powered international bodies involved in tackling girl child issues, it is tempting to think that the ugly acts of systemic violence, abuse and neglect against the girl child are behind us in the 21st Century.

To think that we are once again reminding ourselves that certain cultural and traditional beliefs concerning the girl child remain unbroken in some societies, is not only disturbing but alarming. It is even more distressing that the cases of girl child abuse and molestations across the world make it obvious how much society has tolerated the issue without a firm stand to stop the menace. Though tremendous efforts have been made by governments over the years to curb the ugly act, little impact has been felt. Practices such as female genital mutilation, early girl child marriage, early pregnancy, girl child labour and many other indices delay the growth and development of the girl child in Nigeria. In contemporary times, the main focus of the ills that affect the girl child is child labour. Child labour refers to the high incidence (occurrence, rate or frequency of a disease, crime or something else) of girls aged 5 – 14 years old, who are involved in economic activities outside education and leisure. The prevalence of girl child labour in Nigeria is largely due to household wealth. Other factors include the educational level of parents, peer pressure and demand factors such as high demand for domestic help and sex workers all contribute to the high incidence of girl child labour in the country. In addition, in many rural and Muslim communities in Northern Nigeria, children are sometimes asked to assist religiously secluded women or mothers to run errands.

Many girls work as house helps, shop helps and street hawkers, and the use of young girls for economic activities exposes them to dangers that sometimes result in sexual harassment, loneliness, rape, anger, lack of proper parental care and exploitation. In addition, the workforce of young girls is not recognised by law and any form of employee benefit is negligible.

In Nigeria, child labour is driven by social, demographic and economic factors such as poverty, loss of employment of parents, death of a parent or guardian, rural-urban migration, large family size and cultural norms such as polygamy. Other drivers include the mal-distribution of schools, poor accessibility, and the high cost of tuition. Recently and especially in the northern part of Nigeria, conflicts and terrorism have caused internal displacement of people and damage to school facilities, thereby pushing more children into child labour. The Chibok girls' experience is top of the list as girls are in most cases targeted by these terror groups for obscure reasons. Also, the mass killings of communities by bandits in northern Nigeria have contributed to creating more orphans and potential victims of child labour.

Starting in the mid-1980s, the adverse economic conditions in

Nigeria, a country where men constitute the majority of the employees in the formal sector, forced many women to increase their engagement in the informal but labourintensive sector, in order to supplement household income. Strategies undertaken by women in the informal sector include working long hours in the markets and using their children as hawkers of their goods.

Nigerian scholars have discovered that Nigerians were plunged into great economic hardship since the beginning of the economic intervention programme known as the Structural Adjustment Programme (SAP). Nigerians went through a period of economic hardship where families had to improvise new strategies to survive, such as children being trafficked and sent to the cities as house girls and house boys (domestic staff) or to do other menial jobs and make a living.

To curb this ugly trend in Nigeria, the government of President Olusegun Obasanjo in 2003, enacted the Child Rights Act to protect children from being exploited and denied their rights as minors. Enacting the Child Rights Act is one part of the process, enforcing it is the other part. Up till today, in most rural communities, girl child labour is still on the rise. It is generally believed in some societies in Nigeria that girls are an aid in developing home skills, helping others and family solidarity. Therefore, their main activities include gathering firewood, breaking firewood, grinding pepper and preparing meals, while their male counterparts enjoy all the benefits as a result of family stratification. This resultant socialisation is the major reason girls are preferred to boys in the recruitment of house helps. However, this type of work sometimes impedes the educational prospect of the girl child. In some parts of Northern Nigerian Fulani communities, the girl child helps her mother by hawking milk or other produce from the family farm or made by the mother. Due to the division of labour according to gender in households and also because of socialisation, many Nigerian households prefer to use girls as maids. In return, the wealthier family pays her or her parents or provides her training in a skill of her choosing or a form of basic education. However, the child may face abuse and sexual assault from the household. In some instances, some of the girls are under the age of 8. In Nigeria, many of the girls are from the Southern and Middle Belt regions.

The demand for domestic help in Nigeria and nearby African countries has increased the incidence of child trafficking. This process is enhanced by the invisibility of girls in domestic work because it is considered normal in many urban households. Organised networks procure child labour in the Southern states including Rivers, Akwa Ibom, Imo, Cross River, Ekiti, and Oyo. The children are then transported to other states for domestic work.

Many girls below the age of 15 engage in the vending of goods on roads, carriage of goods to customers and begging for alms. On average, more primary and secondary school-age girls engage in street trading than boys. The young girls choose specific routes and road junctions to vend goods before returning home in the evening. Apart from hawking, some girls also engage in street begging sometimes known as *Almajeri* in the North. About 8 percent of girl hawkers have been subjected to sexual abuse, including cases of rape and sexual violence. Young girls are also exposed to adult challenges and deviant behaviour at an early age with no time to attend school, go to class and complete school work.

Apart from exposure to health risks, child abuse and sexual assault, girl child labour in Nigeria has led to an increase in adolescent-age commercial sex work and exposing girls to the dangers of street life at an early age. Some young girls are trafficked by organised networks who lie to the girls and their parents that they will be housemaids in the cities, whereas some are flown to foreign countries as commercial sex workers. A recent study by the U.S. Department of Labour shows that 31 percent of Nigerian children (around 14,000,000 children) aged 5 to 14 years old are working children who engage in forced labour in various sectors. According to the International

Labour Organization, over 15 million children in Nigeria are estimated to be child labourers. According to the Department's List of Goods Produced by Child Labour or Forced Labour, instances of child labour have been observed in the agricultural sector where children participate in the production of cocoa, cassava, sand and in the mining industry where they mine, quarry and crush gravel and granite.

Another major debacle the girl child faces in Nigeria is early marriage. This is a serious problem that some girls, as opposed to boys, face. The practice of giving away girls for marriage at the age of 11, 12 or 13, after which they must start to produce children, is prevalent among certain ethnic groups in Nigeria. The principal reasons for this practice are in most cases the girls' virginity and the bride price. Young girls are less likely to have had sexual contact and thus are believed to be virgins upon marriage. This condition raises the status of the girl child's family, as well as the dowry to be paid by the husband's family. In some cases, virginity is verified by female relatives before marriage. Child marriage robs a girl of her period of childhood, which is necessary to develop physically, emotionally and psychologically.

Early marriage inflicts great emotional stress on the girl child, as she is removed from her parent's home to that of her husband and in-laws. Her husband, who will invariably be many years her senior, will have little in common with the young teenager. It is with this strange man that she has to develop an intimate emotional and physical relationship. She is obliged to have intercourse, although physically she might not be fully developed. Girls from communities where early marriages occur are also victims of son preferential treatment and will probably be malnourished and consequently have stunted physical growth.

# Chapter Three
## Child marriage

Child marriage in Nigeria is an issue that has prevailed in the Northern part of the country and some parts of Nigeria. This practice is backed by religious sentiments in some regions and cultural beliefs in other parts of the country. In all, child marriage is a human rights violation that prevents girls from obtaining an education, enjoying optimal health, maturing and ultimately choosing their life partners. In most cases, child marriage is driven by poverty and has many effects on girls' health such as the increased risk for sexually transmitted diseases (STDs), cervical cancer, death during childbirth and obstetric fistulas. Girls' offsprings are at increased risk of premature birth and death as neonates, infants or children.

Child marriage and child betrothal customs occur in various times and places, and it is a situation whereby children are given out in matrimony, before marriageable age and often before puberty. Today, such customs are widespread in parts of Africa, Nigeria, Asia, Oceania and South America. In former times, they occurred also in Europe. Child marriage, defined as the marriage of a child under 18 years of age, is an ancient and worldwide custom. Other terms applied to child marriage include *early marriage* and *child bride.* Early marriage could be seen as vague because what is early for one person may be late for another. Cultures have also helped to shape the marriage practices obtainable today. For instance, among the Fulani nation, marriage is mostly based on endogamy; which entails that the first choice of a marriage partner is a patrilateral parallel cousin. Men are also allowed to inherit the assets of deceased family members, including their widows. Another form of marriage that is predominant among the Hausa-Fulani is marriage by the betrothal of female children to adult males. In this part of the country, child marriage is a traditional cultural practice backed up by Islam.

In another scenario, the practice of child marriage is still in place among the Gbagyi people in North Central Nigeria. Typically, initiation into marital life for a male Gbagyi begins between the ages of 15 to 18, as boys within this age bracket are considered capable of producing offspring. As for the case of the female Gbagyi child, betrothment is considered for her between the early ages of 8 and 10. This is due to the expectation that the girl will be ripe for marriage by the time her dowry payment is completed. The Sukur tribe in North East Adamawa state is a clannish society that has practised marital customs that puts the lives of the girl child at risk. In their practice, the Sukurs are exogamous and thus men of different clans marry each other's daughters.

The levirate is also practised within the clan; which is to say that if a man dies and his widow is willing, his brother and potentially any clan brother inherits his house and with it the responsibility of looking after his wife or wives and young children. The hazard of this system of marriage is associated with the insecurities surrounding the girl child in such situations.

Thus, in other words, child marriage could be seen as being a complex issue in Nigeria. It could be viewed differently depending on the context and based on cultural and religious differences, regional and ethnic disparities, among others. Child marriage could therefore be seen as a protective mechanism against premarital sexual activity, unintended pregnancies and sexually transmitted diseases (STDs). The latter concern is even greater in this era of HIV/AIDS.

Child marriage, a global scourge that is practised in many parts of the world, remains prevalent in Africa, including Nigeria and is deeply entrenched in culture and religion. It is not uncommon to find girls below the age of 12 years being betrothed to marriage, especially in the northern part of the country. These girls are given away in marriage without their consent, and this denies them the basic human rights of children and puts them in disadvantaged positions.

However, the major cause of early marriage has been attributed to poverty and based on the Nigeria Demographic and Health Survey (NDHS) of 2013, 58.2 percent of Nigerian girls get married before they turn 18 years old. Moreover, from 2014 to 2020, 16 percent and 43 percent of girls aged 15 and 18 years of age were married respectively.

Many girls are married off by the time they are 15, and some girls are married off as early as age 9. Girls are extremely susceptible to disease and domestic violence and have restricted access to education due to the early age at which they give birth and begin caring for their children. One popular source of legislation that was first brought forward in 1991 and became a national law in 2003, is the Child Rights Act. This Act provides that in all matters involving a child, which may come before a court for adjudication; the best interest of the child is the paramount consideration. Among other factors to protect children from abuses and discrimination, Sections 21 and 23 of the Act made it illegal to marry off a child below the age of 18. If a husband consummates a marriage with a child, it is considered rape.

The Child Rights Act competes with Sharia law in some states as well as with customs and cultural expectations in different regions. The Child Rights Act has not been enacted in 13 of Nigeria's 36 states, where other cultural and religious factors are largely influencing the laws that are enacted. Even in states with laws prohibiting child marriage, these laws have been ineffective since there remains many cases of child marriage. By the provisions of the Child Rights Act, any decision to be made in any proceeding before a court which involves a child; the best interest of the child is the paramount consideration.

Essentially, adherents of Islam argue that it is a religious practice that the Prophet Mohammed exemplified and that his followers should practise. Research however, reveals that child marriage predates Islam. Despite the evidence that child marriage was more of a cultural than religious practice in early Islamic societies, adherents in Nigeria, especially in the North hold fast to the practice and fight any intervention of law or the state to eradicate it. They raise legal provisions to justify their stand.

Research has shown that child marriage is linked to poverty. Moreover, child marriage is increasingly understood as a form of modern slavery and child exploitation. It is generally understood that a child is any person under the age of 18, therefore child marriage is marriage to anyone younger than 18; even if such a union is deemed 'legal'.

Child marriage, generally defined as marriage before the age of 18, is not limited to any country or continent. Generally, girls living in rural areas marry earlier than girls in urban areas. In rural areas of Nigeria, for example, 21 percent of young women, who are now 20 to 24, were married by age 15, as compared to 8 percent in urban areas.

According to Aduradola A. M, the following are some notable issues about child marriage:

1. The causes of child marriage include the following: cultural and social pressure, persecution, forced migration, slavery, financial challenges, religious beliefs, poverty and economic transactions etc.

2. The underlying causes of child marriage also include parental desire to prevent sexual relations before marriage, a lack of education or employment opportunities for girls, and traditional notions of the primary role of girls as wives and mothers.

3. Child marriage is often deployed as a response to the crisis, considered by families and communities to be the best possible means of protecting children. Fear of rape and sexual violence, of unwanted pregnancies outside marriage, family shame and dishonour, homelessness and hunger or starvation were all reported by parents as legitimate reasons for child marriage in

Somaliland, Bangladesh and Niger. Poverty, weak legislative frameworks and enforcement, harmful traditional practices, gender discrimination and lack of alternative opportunities for girls (especially education) are all major drivers of child marriage. Fragility of environment breeds particular fears and anxieties that cause parents to resort to child marriage as a protection against risks (whether real or perceived).

4. Lack of education, the low value placed on girls' education, dropping out of school, gender-based violence (including sexual violence) and early pregnancy can be both causes and consequences of child marriage. In many societies, girls are subject to deep-rooted norms, attitudes and behaviours that assign them a lower status than boys within the household, the community and society at large. These beliefs deny girls their rights and stifle their ability to play equal roles as their male counterparts at home and in the community.

5. The existence of many laws relating to the age of a child and adults in Nigeria is quite conflicting and leads to complications in the adjudication of child marriage. The resultant effect is the complication in legal issues and difficulty in determining and reconciling or fixing the marriageable age of a girl child in Nigeria. We present you with a few of these laws: The Child Rights Act 2003 defines a 'child' as a person who has not attained the age of 18 years. However, according to Article 2

of the Children and Young Persons Act, enacted in the Eastern, Western and Northern regions of Nigeria (hereafter referred to as CYPA), it defines a 'child' as a person under the age of 14 years, while 'young person' means a person who has attained the age of 14 years but is under the age of 17 years. Furthermore, the Immigration Act stipulates that any person below 16 years is a minor, whereas the Matrimonial Causes Act puts the age of maturity at 21. The latter act becomes irrelevant in practice since individual states stipulate their ages for marriage. As for penal responsibility, Article 50 of the Penal Code (North) states, "No act is an offence which is done by a child under 7 years of age or by a child above 7 years of age but under 12 years of age, who has not attained sufficient maturity of understanding to judge the nature and consequence of such an act."

6. Under section 29(4)(a) of the Constitution of the Federal Republic of Nigeria 1999 as amended, 'full age' means the age of 18 years and above. Section 18 of the Marriage Act states that if either party to an intended marriage, not being a widower or widow, is under 21 years of age; the written consent of the father or if he is dead or of unsound mind or absent in Nigeria, of the mother must be produced.

Many of the young girls who are forced into marriage by their parents are completely banned by their parents from going to school, even when some of them excelled at their students. So, it is safe to say that Nigerian bright young people, who could potentially help develop the country, are shut off, and their potential is destroyed forever. Usually, there is a large age gap between a girl and her husband, which can subject her to domestic violence and psychological abuse. This is not to mention the risks that the young girl can meet when she is forced to give birth, the diseases she and her newborn baby can suffer from and even the death of the mother or child.

Most young age marriages happen in the poorer areas, mainly rural ones. We all know that Nigeria is a poor country and most people who live in her rural areas struggle to survive. Many parents who therefore earn very little to maintain normal lives and support their children, choose to force their young daughters into marriage. Girls suffer from it because they often get married against their will. Even though boys do not suffer from this problem as much as girls do, the boys whose families are poor are usually forced into child labour and are subjected to other issues caused by it. In urbanised areas where progressive views on gender inequality is less of a problem, there are still rural areas with ancient beliefs. Often, people are convinced that the boy child is good luck, while the girl child is not, and she can only be used as a future bride. Beliefs in different communities can vary; some of them are based on old religious traditions, and the communities are unwilling to change their lifestyle. As a result of these beliefs, children are given away in marriage.

The lack of proper education is another reason people get their children married at a young age. Many parents choose to look away from the post-marriage life the girl child will have to face, as well as the childbirth complications. Also, due to lack of education, people tend to hold onto many unhealthy traditional beliefs. Since the rate of female harassment continues to grow, many people are concerned about the future of their daughters. Before she becomes an adult, they arrange a marriage with someone much older than her, believing that they are giving her into safe hands and ensuring a trouble-free future for her. Child marriage in Nigeria has an inevitable impact on those who are subjected to it and here are few consequences of this kind of marriage for young girls. Some of them have already been mentioned in this book, but below is a more detailed description of them:

• Early pregnancy: Pregnancy at an early age is harmful to every girl child. The proper age for pregnancy for a girl is at least 18 – 20 years old. If a girl gets pregnant earlier, there is a high risk that she will have to deal with health issues. Sometimes, these health issues can be life-threatening both for the mother and the baby; considering that healthcare in rural areas is not well developed.

• Domestic violence: There are situations where the future husband and in-laws start to blame the girl child for everything after marriage; sometimes even physically abusing her. The child's psychological health is not well-developed, so dealing with the complications of adult life can be too difficult for her to handle. Besides, the violence against her can often result in physical and mental trauma.

• Illiteracy: Once the girl gets married, her parents stop paying for her education, believing that she no longer needs education.

# Chapter Four
## Living with Atrocities

Nigeria is a country of diverse cultures and these different cultures reflect values and beliefs held by members of a community for periods often spanning generations. Every social grouping in this country has specific cultural practices and beliefs; some of which are beneficial to all members, while others are harmful to a specific group, such as women. These harmful cultural practices include female genital mutilation (FGM), child marriage, various taboos or practices that prevent women from controlling their fertility, nutritional taboos and traditional birth practices, son preference and its implications for the status of the girl child, female infanticide; child pregnancy, dowry price etc. Despite their harmful natures, they have an aura of morality in the eyes of those who practise them.

Several reasons are given for the persistent practice of cultural practices that are detrimental to the health and status of women. In the past, neither the governments concerned nor the international community challenged the sinister implications of such practices, which violated the rights to health, life, dignity and personal integrity of the children involved.

Nigeria accounts for the highest cases of female genital mutilation worldwide. This practice is customarily a family tradition that young females aged 0-15 undergo. It is a procedure that involves the cutting or removal of some or all of the external female genitalia. In Nigeria, this practice is most prevalent among the Yoruba people of the South West with Osun State recording 98 percent of cases closely followed by Oyo State with a prevalent rate of 96.8 percent. Cases of FGM are also high in Niger, Rivers, Borno State and Kebbi states.

The international community became wary about treating these issues as a deserving subject for international and national scrutiny and action. Harmful practices such as female genital mutilation were considered sensitive cultural issues that fall within the spheres of women and the family. For a long time, governments and the international community had not expressed sympathy and understanding for women, who due to ignorance endured pain, suffering and even death inflicted on themselves and their female children.

The harmful traditional practices identified in this book are categorised as separate issues, however they are all consequences of the value placed on the girl child by society. They persist in an environment where the girl child has unequal access to education, wealth, health and employment. The girl child in Nigeria has lived with atrocities that stem from traditions, customs and other practices. In this part of the book, we look at some of the practices that degrade the dignity of girls in society.

## Female genital mutilation

Female genital mutilation (FGM) or female circumcision as it is sometimes erroneously referred to, involves the cutting or removal of parts or all of the external female genitalia. It is an age-old practice that is perpetuated in many communities around the world, simply because it is customary. FGM forms an important part of the rites of passage ceremony for some communities, marking the coming of age of the female child. It is believed that by mutilating the female genital organ, her sexuality will be controlled and above all, it is to ensure a woman's virginity before marriage and chastity thereafter. FGM imposes on women and the girl child a catalogue of health complications and untold psychological problems.

The practice of FGM violates, among other international human rights laws, the right of the child to the 'enjoyment of the highest attainable standard of health', as laid down in article 24 (paragraphs 1 and 3) of the Convention on the Rights of the Child. The origin of FGM has not yet been established, but records show that the practice predates Christianity and Islam in the practising communities of today. In ancient Rome, metal rings were passed through the labia minora of slaves to prevent procreation. In medieval England, metal chastity belts were worn by women to prevent promiscuity during their husbands' absence. Evidence from mummified bodies reveal that in ancient Egypt, both excision and infibulations were performed, hence Pharaonic circumcision. In tsarist Russia, as well as nineteenth-century England, France and America, records indicate the practice of clitoridectomy. In England and America, FGM was performed on women as a 'cure' for numerous psychological ailments.

The age at which mutilation is carried out varies from area to area. FGM is performed on infants as young as a few days old, children from 7 to 10 years old and adolescents. Adult women also undergo the procedure as at the time of marriage. Since FGM is performed on infants as well as adults, it can no longer be seen as marking the rites of passage into adulthood or to ensure virginity.

The effects of female genital mutilation have short-term and long-term implications. Haemorrhage, infection and acute pain are the immediate consequences. Keloid formation, infertility as a result of infection, obstructed labour and psychological complications are identified as later effects. In rural areas where untrained traditional birth attendants perform the procedure, complications resulting from deep cuts and infected instruments can cause the death of the girl child.

Most physical complications result from infibulation, although cataclysmic haemorrhage can occur during the removal of the clitoris. Accidental cuts to other organs can also lead to loss of blood. Acute infections are commonplace when such procedures are carried out in unhygienic surroundings and with unsterilised instruments. The application of traditional medicine can lead to infection, resulting in tetanus and general septicaemia, and chronic infection can lead to infertility and anaemia.

Haematocolpos or the inability to pass menstrual blood (because the remaining opening is often too small), can lead to infection of other organs and infertility. Obstetric complications are the most frequent health problems that result from vicious scars in the clitoral zone after excision. These scars open during childbirth and cause the anterior perineum to tear, leading to haemorrhaging that is often difficult to stop. Infibulated women have to be opened, or de-infibulated on delivery of their children, and it is common for them to be reinfibulated after each delivery.

## Son preference

The preference for sons is very high, exists in several cultures and dates back to pre-historic times. It is tied to inheritance and unfortunately, has not succumbed to societal changes but has remained sacrosanct because of the desire for a son to carry on the family name and guarantee the family lineage. One of the principal forms of discrimination and one that has far-reaching implications for women is the preference accorded to the boy child over the girl child. This practice denies the girl child good health, education, recreation, economic opportunities, and the right to choose her partner; thus violating her rights under articles 2, 6, 12, 19, 24, 27 and 28 of the Convention on the Rights of the Child.

Son preference refers to a whole range of values and attitudes that are manifested in many different practices, the common feature of which is a preference for the male child; often with a concomitant neglect of daughters. It may mean that a female child is disadvantaged from birth, it may determine the quality and quantity of parental care and the extent of investment in her development, and it may lead to acute discrimination; particularly in settings where resources are scarce. Although neglect is the rule, in extreme cases, son preference may lead to selective abortion or female infanticide. In many societies, the family lineage is carried on by male children, and the preservation of the family name is guaranteed through son(s). Except in a few countries (e.g. Ethiopia), a girl takes her husband's family name and drops that of her parents. The fear of losing a name therefore prompts families to wish to have a son. Some men marry a second or a third wife to be sure of having a male child. Among many communities in Asia and Africa, sons perform burial rites for their parents. Parents with no male child do not expect to have an appropriate burial to 'secure their peace in the next world.'

In almost all religions, ceremonies are performed by men. Priests, pastors, sheikhs and other religious leaders are men of great status to whom society attaches great importance, and this important role for men obliges parents to wish for a male child. Religious leaders have a major involvement in the perpetuation of son preference. Son preference is universal and not unique to developing countries or rural areas. It is a practice enshrined in the value systems of most societies. In almost all regions, the practice is rooted in culture and the economics of son preference, and these factors play a major role in the low valuation and neglect of female children.

The psychological effect of son preference on women and the girl child is the internalisation of the low value accorded them by society. Scientific evidence of the deleterious effect of son preference on the health of female children is scarce, but abnormal sex ratios in infant and young child mortality rates, in nutritional status indicators and even in population figures show that discriminatory practices are widespread and have serious repercussions. Geographically, there is often a close correspondence between the areas of strong son preference and of health disadvantages for females.

Countless reports the world over have demonstrated that, in societies where son preference is practised, the health of the female child is adversely affected. In some communities in the Asian region where son preference is highly marked, efforts to differentiate a female child from a male child through various socio-economic norms and practices start as early as the foetal stage and continue throughout the entire life cycle.

In these communities, amniocentesis tests and sonography for sex determination have resulted in the abortion of female foetuses. The introduction and expansion of scientific methods of sex detection have led to a revival of female foeticide and infanticide.

**Education**

Access to education by itself is not enough to eliminate values held by society, for such values are in most countries transmitted into educational curricular and textbooks. Women are thus still depicted as passive and domestically oriented, while men are depicted as dominant and as breadwinners. Education does, however offer the female child an improved opportunity to be less dependent on men in later life, as it increases her prospects of obtaining work outside the home.

As laid down in articles 28 and 29 of the Convention on the Rights of the Child, all children have a right to education, and the content of such education should be directed towards the development of the child's personality, talents and mental and physical abilities to their fullest potential. According to the United Nations Children's Fund (UNICEF), the expansion of educational opportunities over the past several decades have affected girls, although this has not been a result of a deliberate policy to reduce gender disparities in educational access. Girls' education, measured by gross primary school enrolment ratios, has improved substantially in the Middle East and North Africa region, for example.

Nevertheless, in 1990, the region still had 44 million illiterate mothers, a large and increasing backlog left over from the times of low enrolment levels. Differences in primary school enrolment levels for boys and girls and competition between them are still significant in several countries. In countries where overall enrolment is much lower than desired, girls are particularly disadvantaged. Although in many countries where school drop-out rates are steadily falling, they continue to be higher among girls than among boys.

The reasons for the high drop-out rate among girls are poverty, child marriage, helping parents with housework and agricultural work, the distance of schools from home, the high cost of schooling, parents' illiteracy and indifference, and the lack of a positive educational climate. Girls begin school very late and withdraw with the onset of puberty. Parents do not see the benefits of girls' education, because girls are given away in marriage to serve the husband's family. On the other hand, sons are given priority. In certain countries, enrolment rates for girls have declined despite attempts to increase them.

**Recreation and work opportunities**

Paragraph 1 of Article 31 of the Convention on the Rights of the Child, recognises 'the right of the child to rest and leisure and to engage in play and recreational activities.' However, from an early age, girls from rural and poor urban homes are burdened with domestic tasks and child care, which leaves them no time to play. Studies have shown that recreation plays a vital part in a child's emotional and mental development. And, when the time for play is found by girls, it often takes place near the home. Young boys, however, have fewer demands made of them and are allowed to engage in activities outside the home.

The status of girls is linked to that of women and their exploitation. A woman's work never ends, especially in rural areas and in poor urban households. The Convention on the Elimination of All Forms of Discrimination against Women calls for the elimination of discrimination against women in the field of employment; 'to ensure, on a basis of equality of men and women, the same rights' (Article 11, paragraph 1). It also calls upon states to ensure that women in rural areas have access to agricultural credit and loans, marketing facilities, appropriate technology and equal treatment in land and agrarian reform (Article 14, paragraph 2) (g).

Evidence indicates however, that as girls grow older they face discriminatory treatment in gaining access to economic opportunities. Major inequalities persist in employment, access to credit, inheritance rights, marriage laws and other socio-economic dispensations. Compared with men, women have fewer opportunities for paid employment and less access to skill training that would make such employment possible. Women are usually restricted to low-pay and casual jobs or informal activities. Landlessness has increased among women, and the number of women cultivators have declined in some regions, partly due to increased mechanisation of agriculture.

Female infanticide, gender bias or son preference places the female child in a disadvantageous position from birth. In some communities, particularly in Asia, the practice of infanticide ensures that some female children have no life at all, thus violating the basic right to life laid down in Article 6 of the Convention on the Rights of the Child. Selective abortion, foeticide and infanticide all occur because the female child is not valued by her culture or because certain economic and legislative acts have ruled her life worthless. In India, for example, infanticide was formally legislated during British rule, after centuries of practice in some communities. However, recent reports have shown that there is a revival. In certain parts of India and Pakistan, women are still considered unnecessary evils.

In the past, when victorious armies took their revenge on defeated communities, women were raped as part of the spoils of war. Subsequently, these communities resorted to killing their daughters at birth or when the enemy was advancing, to spare the female population and community shame. Modern techniques such as amniocentesis and ultrasound tests have given women greater power to detect the gender of their babies, in time to abort them. Illegal abortion, particularly of female foetuses, either self-inflicted or performed by unskilled birth attendants, under poor sanitary conditions has led to increased maternal mortality; particularly in South-east Asia.

Female foeticide is an emerging problem in some parts of India, and the government has introduced a bill in Parliament to ban the use of amniocentesis for gender-determination purposes. Such misuse of amniocentesis is also prohibited in the States of Maharashtra, Punjab, Rajasthan and Haryana; where the problem is more prevalent.

## Early Marriage and Dowry

Early marriage is another serious problem which some girls face. The practice of giving away girls for marriage at the age of 11, 12 or 13, after which they must start producing children, is prevalent among certain ethnic groups in Asia and Africa. The principal reasons for this practice are the girls' virginity and bride price. Young girls are less likely to have had sexual contact and thus are believed to be virgins upon marriage; this condition raises the family status as well as the dowry to be paid by the husband. In some cases, virginity is verified by female relatives before marriage.

Child marriage robs a girl of her childhood, which is necessary to develop physically, emotionally and psychologically. It inflicts great emotional stress as the young girl is removed from her parent's home to that of her husband and in-laws. Her husband, who will invariably be many years her senior, will have little in common with the young teenager. It is with this strange man that she has to develop an intimate emotional and physical relationship. She is obliged to have intercourse, even though physically she might not be fully developed. Girls from communities where early marriages occur are also victims of son preferential treatment and will probably be malnourished and consequently have stunted physical growth. Neglect of and discrimination against daughters, particularly in societies with strong son preferences, also contribute to the early marriage of girls. It has been generally recognised at United Nations seminars on traditional practices that affect children and women based on research, that child marriage devalues women in some societies and that the practice continues as a result of son preference.

In some countries, girls as young as a few months old are promised to male suitors for marriage. Girls are also fattened up, groomed, adorned with jewels and kept in seclusion to make them attractive so that they can be married off to the highest bidder.

**Early pregnancy, nutritional taboos and practices related to child delivery**

Early pregnancy can have harmful consequences for both young mothers and their babies. According to UNICEF, no girl should become pregnant before the age of 18, because she is not yet physically ready to bear children. Babies of mothers younger than 18 tend to be born prematurely and have low body weight. Such babies are more likely to die in the first year of life. The risk to the young mother's health is also great.

# Chapter Five
## Girl Child Policy in Nigeria

Nigeria's underdevelopment regarding the status of their women, due to a long history of colonial exploitation and oppression, has brought about a distortion of her economic, educational, religious, cultural, social, ideological and social orientation. The social role of women in Nigeria varies according to religious, cultural and geographic factors.

However, many Nigerian cultures see women solely as mothers, sisters, daughters and wives. For instance, women in Northern Nigeria are more likely to be secluded in the home than women in Southern Nigeria, who tend to participate more in public life. In Nigeria, widows experience illtreatment from their in-laws which include forcing them to drink the remnant water after bathing the dead husband, sleeping on the bare floor, wearing a black gown, and denying them inheritance from the wealth of their deceased husband. The unimaginable inequality and danger that faces the girl child in Nigeria today has risen to an alarming proportion. The statistics as mentioned above, are of course, warped depending on cases reported to the agency or who is on the podium. It is high time the government grasped the dangers associated with child marriage as one notable factor that slows down the progress and development of the nation. Indeed, it is disheartening to hear some underlying assumptions among the masses that it is a waste of time and money to educate the girl-child.

Both the policy makers in government and those who share the above view should wake up from their slumber and tackle this noxious practice against the girl child. It is striking to read a report in an edition of *The Economist* magazine that nations that fail women end up as failed nations, while those that place the required premium on educating women have recorded numerous technological advancements and scaled economic frontiers. An example is not farfetched as our nation Nigeria, is a witness of her woeful failure on women affairs and her tilt towards a failed state. The Beijing conference in 1995 set out to reshape the position of women in society, after what seemed like ageless wisdom to continue keeping women in the background.

Today, it is disheartening that the girl child continues to suffer policy abandonment and social and cultural prejudices in some regions and communities in Nigeria. Regrettably, in some other places across the world, the girl child is not allowed to be born as girls are selectively aborted, a situation that has led to a skewed sex ratio, and millions of young men seem doomed to remain single. Therefore, frustrated young men are more susceptible to committing violent crimes or joining rebel groups.

The government must be seen to walk its talk and make the laws bite by criminalising offences against the girl child. In the same breath, it behoves every citizen to play his/her part in the progress and development of the girl child for a better and safer society. It has been over one decade since the world began to mark the *International Day of the Girl Child (IDGC)*, which has drawn attention to issues that concern girls in Nigeria and across the world.

State governments, policymakers and the general public have lent their voices to the campaign for a better life for the girl child, yet investments in girls' rights remain limited and female children continue to face challenges that prevent them from fulfilling their potential. According to the World Health Organisation (WHO), adolescence is a critical period that can determine the trajectory of girls' lives. It is the stage at which key investments and support can set girls on a path toward empowerment or when discrimination, recurrent constraints, harmful practices and violence can send them down a negative spiral. These come with lifelong consequences not just for themselves, but for societies and future generations.

However, the girl child all over the world has encountered

some forms of challenges as a result of cultural, religious, political and social beliefs. These challenges, quite naturally, in some cases, have made the girl-child an 'endangered' specie. Some of these challenges include child marriage, teenage pregnancy, violence at home and school, lack of funding, child/domestic labour, poor sanitation and facilities, insecurity, wars and natural disasters, disabilities and 'just because they are girls' as part of cultural discrimination, among others. To find solutions to these, agencies came together under the instrumentality of the Millennium Development Goals and finally, the Sustainable Development Goals (SDGs) to see that the girl-child is liberated from everything hindering her. It is in the light of this that October 11 was declared the *International Day of the Girl Child* to celebrate female folks in general. Scholars, artists and Non Governmental Agencies have advocated the empowerment of the girl child using the tools of technology.

In 2003, Nigeria adopted the Child Rights Act to domesticate the Convention on the Rights of the Child. The Child Rights Act of 2003 expands the human rights bestowed on citizens in Nigeria's 1999 constitution to children. Although this law was passed at the federal level, it is only effective if state assemblies also codify the law.

The bill was first introduced in 2002 but did not pass because of opposition from the Supreme Council for Shari'a. The act was officially passed into law in 2003 by Former President Chief Olusegun Obasanjo as the Child Rights Act 2003, in large part because of the media pressure that national stakeholders and international organisations put on the National Assembly.

The Child Rights Act itself is 230 pages long and contains 278 different sections.

Part I – mandates that where a child is concerned, their best interest is to take precedence. It goes on to state that the parent or legal guardian is obligated to fulfil the duty to give the child basic protection.

Part II – specifies that the Article IV of Nigeria's 1999 constitution and any other federal law which details fundamental rights should be seen as being part of the act. This article details the rights, freedoms and responsibilities of children. It goes on to state specific rights for children including the right to survival, a name, family life, private life, dignity, recreation, cultural activities, health services and education.

Part Ill – discusses how a child shall be protected. These include protection from child marriage as well as punishments for the act to the adult parties involved. Other protections include, not being harmed (including being marked with tattoos) or from sexual violence, being shielded from exploitative labour or being enlisted in any military operation.

Part IV – lists the reasons when a child assessment order may be sought as well as the reasons and duration for which emergency protection orders shall be given to a child. It also made clear the obligation of a state government when it is disclosed to it that a child is being harmed.

Part V – indicates the circumstances in which a child shall be brought to court to determine if they need protection. This part also stipulates the type of person who shall be allowed to make such a decision using the guidelines detailed in this section.

Part VI – enumerates the ways and manner in which a court must proceed after a child assessment order is made.

Part VII – allows for the court to use paternity tests to make decisions in civil proceedings when it is unclear who the parents of a child are.

Part VIII – shows how decisions should be made about the custody of a child.

Part IX – details who is allowed guardianship and how guardianship may be transferred from one adult to another over a child.

Part X – establishes how a child becomes a ward of the court; that there may be payments required of a previous guardian for the 'maintenance' of their child, and the rules regarding how a child may be released back into the custody of a guardian.

Part XI – outlines the circumstances in which a child may be fostered, how an adult may apply to foster a child, and the rules the adult fostering the child must adhere to.

Part XII – requires that each state of Nigeria create a system for adoption services. This section also outlines the process of applying for adoption and stipulates that the person wishing to adopt a child must reside within the state where the child already lives.

Part XIII – creates a system of family courts with two levels, establishes a right to legal counsel for all children, and devises safeguards (such as the withholding of the child's name, school pictures or any identifying features) within a trial which is meant to protect the child.

Part XIV – mandates that every state creates a registry which shall track the names of the children being supervised as well as the names of the individual nannies or daycare providers who are tasked with watching the children. This clause also grants the government the power to inspect any premise in which 'child minding' occurs.

Part XV – outlines the instances where a state government is required to step in to protect the welfare of children.

Part XVI to XVIII – indicates the types of housing that may be established to house children: community homes (or housing for children who are under the care of the government or not), voluntary homes and registered children's homes.

Part XIX – establishes that a minister may grant the inspectionof children's homes for the reasons listed in the clause.

Part XX – grants children the right to privacy in the court system. This section also makes it clear that children are to be tried through the child justice system and not the courts where adults are tried. It is indicated that within the Nigerian Police Force, there must be individuals trained specifically to handle children. From a child's arrest to their treatment in an institution, this section outlines the procedures.

Part XXI – shows how 'supervision officers' are appointed as well as the duties of the specially appointed officers.

Part XXII – specifies that this act allows for the minister to create specific institutions meant to meet the needs of children.

These centres include (but are not limited to): Children's Residential Centres, Emergency Protection Centres, and Children Correction Centres.

Part XXIII – creates the National Child Rights Implementation Committee which must consist of one representative from fourteen of Nigeria's governmental bodies. The function of the committee is to take actions which will lead to the observance of the Act itself as well as other human rights treaties Nigeria has signed onto.

Part XXIV – is labelled as 'Miscellaneous' and touches on some of the legal implications corporations may face for not following this Act. This section also further defines terms.

As of 2016, the Child Rights Act was codified into law in 24 of Nigeria's 36 states, with Enugu being the most recent to enact the law in December 2016. To enforce the Act, The National Child Rights Implementation Committee was created. Committees were also established for some of the states which have ratified the Act. The committee listed five top priorities for addressing the needs of children: establishing safe water supply and sanitation, working on the HIV/AIDS epidemic, creating job opportunities for women so they are better able to take care of their children, providing universal basic education, and making the primary health care system better. A 2010 report notes that the capacity for monitoring and sufficiently implementing the Act is low.

Another way in which the Child Rights Act proves difficult to enforce is that it contradicts other national laws. Even though the Child Rights Act defines a child as a person that is under 18 years old, this conflicts with another Nigerian Law, the Young Person's Act, which designates a child as an individual below the age of 14. In contrast, The Young Person's Acts deems individuals aged 14 to 17 as 'young people'.

The definitions created by these two separate laws are in tension with each other and pose issues in matters of interpretation. Although the provisions within the Child Rights Act should be seen as overruling any other law, the fact that the Child Rights Act is not ratified in all Nigerian States makes it difficult.

There are two main ways religious groups approach the idea of human rights. The first is by thinking of human rights as divinely granted by God. For those who practice Islam, this can be seen in the symmetry between some of the rights outlined in the Universal Declaration of Human Rights and the Quran. When it comes to the human rights of children, there are passages in the Quran and Hadith which are compatible with the Child Rights Act of 2003. For example, the right to custody or guardianship is discussed in Q 65:7, and the right to education is expressed in Tirmidhi, Hadith 218. A second way in which religious groups may see human rights is as an imposition of the West that is contrary to religious or cultural practices.

Although there are many ways in which Islamic Law is compatible with The Child Rights Act, as outlined above, there are five main clauses which are contrary to Islamic law within the 2003 Act. First is the clause about child marriage within Part Ill. In the Child Rights Act, it is stated that any marriage that a child takes part in shall be considered unlawful because children are not capable of being part of a valid marriage contract. This law contradicts the Islamic doctrine that a girl's father may betroth her without obtaining her consent. Second, in Part VIII, it is established that once a child is legally adopted, his adoptive parent or parents become solely responsible for him, thereby taking away the birth parent's rights to make any decisions regarding the child. The concept of the birth parents relinquishing all rights to the child is in tension with Surrah 33:4-5, where it is stated that children should remain attached to their birth parents by name.

Third, it is upheld in Part VIII of the Child Rights Act that in the instance that a child's parents are not married to each other before they have children, either the mother or father can claim custody of the child. For many in the Islamic community, when a child is born out of wedlock it is a serious matter, and this clause in the Child Rights Act can be seen as much too casual. The fourth subject of tension between the Child Rights Act and the Islamic community is the subject of guardianship or custody as stipulated in Part IX of the act. Islamic law generally regards the mother as the rightful steward of a child. However, the Child Rights Act considers the welfare and wants of the child as well as the capability and wishes of the parents when deciding on who is going to be the child's guardian. Lastly, the issue of withholding corporal punishment from children, as brought up in Part XX of the Child Rights Act is thought by some to be not only un-lslamic but also un-African.

# Chapter Six
## Hope for the Future

Teenage girls in Nigeria who belong to a group called *It's Never Your Fault* are fighting for the right not to be married before the age of 18, as stipulated in Part Ill of the Child Rights Act. Currently, a loophole in the constitution stipulates that upon marriage, a girl is to be regarded as an adult, regardless of the child's age when she got married. As at 2018, the group (*It's Never Your Fault*) has gathered over 150,000 signatures for a petition which demands that the government change the age of consent to 18 years old.

Recently, we have seen a surge of girl child education debates surrounding primary, secondary, tertiary and health/safety education in particular for girls and young women. These issues and debates on the education of the girl child are not lost on the Nigerian nation as well, as it is estimated that Nigeria has the largest population of youth in the world with girls being up to 40% of the number.

*"Over the past 10 years, there has been increased attention on issues that matter to girls amongst governments, policymakers and the general public, and more opportunities for girls to have their voices heard on the global stage. Yet, investments in girls' rights remain limited and girls continue to*

*confront a myriad of challenges to fulfilling their potential; made worse by concurrent crises of climate change, COVID-19 and humanitarian conflict. Girls around the world continue to face unprecedented challenges to their education, their physical and mental wellness, and the protections needed for a life without violence."* – UNICEF

There are presently millions of school-age girls in Nigeria who are out of school, yet we agree that the Nigerian girl child needs to be educated now. It is her right to acquire the knowledge and skills needed to advance her status for social interactions and selfimprovement. When a girl child is given safety education that is human dignity-based alongside curriculum-based education, it prepares her to face realities in society and teaches her to become a good person, wife, mother or any other career she may choose to embrace. Little girls are the future, thus when we teach them to accept their God-given identities and educate them on safety, we help them to find themselves and lead the way. Whilst educating girls and teaching them the safety of abstaining from body abuse, we are saving lives and building stronger families, communities and economies for the future. This is because an educated female population that makes wise choices increases a country's productivity and fuels economic growth.

In discussing girls' rights, one question that is paramount is, "Would a good father or mother encourage their pre-teen or teenage child to indulge in safe sex (and most probably come out damaged) when the child is still immature for the emotional stress, which accompanies an active indulgence in safe sex?" The answer is obvious.

It is therefore sad and outrightly disgusting that rather than promote abstinence for unmarried teens who are still children by the way, some activists go about to tell them that they are free to use condoms and have safe sex. Equally horrifying is the offering of 'services' like hormonal implants and abortions for teenage girls, by certain groups who claim to protect the sexual rights of the girl child. These groups pretend not to know that unlike animals, human beings are not governed by instincts; they are beings who are perfectly able to control their urges and take responsibility for them. Therefore, it is the primary responsibility of parents to teach their children age-appropriate sexuality education, not school teachers who more often than not (from recent happenings in Nigeria) lure the school pupils into sexual promiscuity without realising it, all in the name of sex education. Age-appropriate sexuality education is what should be taught to pupils and students, not just sex education.

It is important that teachers should strengthen the moral values handed down by parents to their children and where these values are non-existent, to teach them afresh to children. We care about the girl child and desire to protect her from terrible practices and predators. Our message this year is this: *It's time to protect the girl child's right to a bright future.* Yes! We work to promote her God-given dignity in the home, at school and in society.

# ABOUT THE BOOK

*Dilemma of the Nigerian Girl Child* is a thought-provoking book that sheds light on the challenges faced by young girls in Nigeria. Through a blend of personal stories and expert insights, this book explores the cultural and social pressures that hinder the growth and development of Nigeria's female youth, through issues such as child marriage, limited access to education and poverty. This book is a must-read for anyone looking to better understand the struggles of the Nigerian girl child, and the impact these challenges have on their lives and communities. With a focus on hope and empowerment, *The Dilemma of the Nigerian Girl Child* provides a roadmap for positive change and a brighter future for generations to come.

# ABOUT THE AUTHOR

Queen Jennifer Ephraim is a Nigerian model, public speaker and award-winning beauty queen. She graduated from Adonai University with a B.Sc in International Relations and French and holds certifications in Human Resources, Project Management and Customer Care. At 21 years old, she founded the *Jennifer Ephraim Foundation*, which empowers children and women in Nigeria, with plans to expand to other African countries. Queen Jennifer is passionate about helping the less-privileged and promoting education and empowerment through her foundation.